Progress Is A Progress

Progress Is A Progress

90 Days Of Life Changing Quotes

Dwight Solomon

Original and modified cover art by Steve Jurvetson and CoverDesignStudio.com

ISBN-13: 978-1519174215
ISBN-10: 1519174217

Progress Is A Process

CONTENTS

ACKNOWLEDGEMENTS

INTRODUCTION

Acknowledgements

I want to thank GOD the supreme creator of the universe for his guidance protection and intervention in my life and affairs. Also to all my family and friends for your support and motivation. Thank you all.

Introduction

I love powerful quotes to me they are instant motivators. Especially when the quote is addressing something I am dealing with or going through at the time, or if the author is a person I love and admire. A good quote can instantly get a person positive and on track.

So I put together a book of some of my personal favorites, but more importantly quotes that will light your fire instantly to balance and repel the massive amount of negativity and hardship that we all deal with every day. Like I said in my book Progress Is a Process: An Inspirational Story and a Guide to Life Mastery. I discus the reasons I believe it is a must to read positive quotes daily and expose ourselves to motivational information daily. To try to balance and overcome all the negativity coming from all directions, like social media, jobs, TV, relationships literally everywhere we turn there something bad happening, just happened or about to happen. Have your defense ready have your quotes in hand so you can stay prepared to handle anything. So here is 90 days of inspirational quotes to light your fire.

DAY 1

Don't be afraid to give your best to what seemingly are small jobs. Every time you conquer one it makes you that much stronger. If you do the little jobs well, the big ones will tend to take care of themselves.

Dale Carnegie

DAY 2

You've done it before and you can do it now. See the positive possibilities. Redirect the substantial energy of your frustration and turn it into positive, effective, unstoppable determination.

Ralph Marston

DAY 3

Start with God - the first step in learning is bowing down to God; only fools thumb their noses at such wisdom and learning.

King Solomon

DAY 4

We were all born with a certain degree of power. The key to success is discovering this innate power and using it daily to deal with whatever challenges come our way.

Les Brown

DAY 5

Being deeply loved by someone gives you strength, while loving someone deeply gives you courage.

Lao Tzu

DAY 6

I have decided to stick with love. Hate is too great a burden to bear.

Martin Luther King, Jr.

DAY 7

Love and compassion are necessities, not luxuries. Without them humanity cannot survive.

Dalai Lama

DAY 8

Strength and growth come only through continuous effort and struggle.

Napoleon Hill

DAY 9

Good actions give strength to ourselves and inspire good actions in others.

Plato

DAY 10

Only one who devotes himself to a cause with his whole strength and soul can be a true master. For this reason mastery demands all of a person.

Albert Einstein

DAY 11

Rivers, ponds, lakes and streams - they all have different names, but they all contain water. Just as religions do - they all contain truths.

Muhammad Ali

DAY 12

If you have no confidence in self, you are twice defeated in the race of life.

Marcus Garvey

DAY 13

When I admire the wonders of a sunset or the beauty of the moon, my soul expands in the worship of the creator.

Mahatma Gandhi

DAY 14

Life is one big road with lots of signs. So when you riding through the ruts, don't complicate your mind. Flee from hate, mischief and jealousy. Don't bury your thoughts, put your vision to reality. Wake Up and Live!

Bob Marley

DAY 15

You may not always have a comfortable life and you will not always be able to solve all of the world's problems at once but don't ever underestimate the importance you can have because history has shown us that courage can be contagious and hope can take on a life of its own.

Michelle Obama

DAY 16

Let us remember: One book, one pen, one child, and one teacher can change the world.

Malala Yousafzai

DAY 17

Forgiveness is about empowering yourself, rather than empowering your past.

T. D. Jakes

DAY 18

Karma is experience, and experience creates memory, and memory creates imagination and desire, and desire creates karma again. If I buy a cup of coffee, that's karma. I now have that memory that might give me the potential desire for having cappuccino, and I walk into Starbucks, and there's karma all over again.

Deepak Chopra

DAY 19

God, our Creator, has stored within our minds and personalities, great potential strength and ability. Prayer helps us tap and develop these powers.

A. P. J. Abdul Kalam

DAY 20

One who neglects or disregards the existence of earth, air, fire, water and vegetation disregards his own existence which is entwined with them.

Mahavira

DAY 21

Passion is energy. Feel the power that comes from focusing on what excites you.

Oprah Winfrey

DAY 22

The energy of the mind is the essence
of life.

Aristotle

DAY 23

A good deed here, a good deed there, a good thought here, a good comment there, all added up to my career in one way or another.

Sidney Poitier

DAY 24

When you love and accept yourself, when you know who really cares about you, and when you learn from your mistakes, then you stop caring about what people who don't know you think.

Beyonce Knowles

DAY 25

If you fall behind, run faster. Never give up, never surrender, and rise up against the odds.

Jesse Jackson

DAY 26

I'd be more frightened by not using whatever abilities I'd been given. I'd be more frightened by procrastination and laziness.

Denzel Washington

DAY 27

I love those who can smile in trouble, who can gather strength from distress, and grow brave by reflection. 'Tis the business of little minds to shrink, but they whose heart is firm, and whose conscience approves their conduct, will pursue their principles unto death.

Leonardo da Vinci

DAY 28

When adversity strikes, that's when you have to be the most calm. Take a step back, stay strong, stay grounded and press on.

LL Cool J

DAY 29

As long as we persevere and endure,
we can get anything we want.

Mike Tyson

DAY 30

I don't know what my calling is, but I want to be here for a bigger reason. I strive to be like the greatest people who have ever lived.

Will Smith

DAY 31

It is in your moments of decision that
your destiny is shaped.

Tony Robbins

DAY 32

Happiness doesn't depend on any external conditions; it is governed by our mental attitude.

Dale Carnegie

DAY 33

If you can dream it, you can do it.

Walt Disney

DAY 34

The strong man is the one who is able to intercept at will the communication between the senses and the mind.

Napoleon Bonaparte

DAY 35

The resistance that you fight physically in the gym and the resistance that you fight in life can only build a strong character.

Arnold Schwarzenegger

DAY 36

Be happy for this moment. This moment is your life.

Omar Khayyam

DAY 37

Let us always meet each other with smile, for the smile is the beginning of love.

Mother Teresa

DAY 38

Your work is going to fill a large part of your life, and the only way to be truly satisfied is to do what you believe is great work. And the only way to do great work is to love what you do. If you haven't found it yet, keep looking. Don't settle. As with all matters of the heart, you'll know when you find it.

Steve Jobs

DAY 39

We know what we are, but know not
what we may be.

William Shakespeare

DAY 40

Change your thoughts and you
change your world.

Norman Vincent Peale

DAY 41

There is only one way to happiness and that is to cease worrying about things which are beyond the power of our will.

Epictetus

DAY 42

If you always put limit on everything you do, physical or anything else. It will spread into your work and into your life. There are no limits. There are only plateaus, and you must not stay there, you must go beyond them.

Bruce Lee

DAY 43

Memories of our lives, of our works and our deeds will continue in others.

Rosa Parks

DAY 44

Don't limit yourself. Many people limit themselves to what they think they can do. You can go as far as your mind lets you. What you believe, remember, you can achieve.

Mary Kay Ash

DAY 45

Someone is sitting in the shade today because someone planted a tree a long time ago.

Warren Buffett

DAY 46

If we did all the things we are capable of, we would literally astound ourselves.

Thomas A. Edison

DAY 47

If you accept the expectations of others, especially negative ones, then you never will change the outcome.

Michael Jordan

DAY 48

Let us dream of tomorrow where we can truly love from the soul, and know love as the ultimate truth at the heart of all creation.

Michael Jackson

DAY 49

Life shrinks or expands in proportion to one's courage.

Anais Nin

DAY 50

When you reach the end of your rope, tie a knot in it and hang on.

Franklin D. Roosevelt

DAY 51

Learning how to be still, to really be still and let life happen - that stillness becomes a radiance.

Morgan Freeman

DAY 52

Every great dream begins with a dreamer. Always remember, you have within you the strength, the patience, and the passion to reach for the stars to change the world.

Harriet Tubman

DAY 53

In order to succeed, we must first believe that we can.

Nikos Kazantzakis

DAY 54

Once you replace negative thoughts with positive ones, you'll start having positive results.

Willie Nelson

DAY 55

Positive thinking will let you do everything better than negative thinking will.

Zig Ziglar

DAY 56

You've done it before and you can do it now. See the positive possibilities. Redirect the substantial energy of your frustration and turn it into positive, effective, unstoppable determination.

Ralph Marston

DAY 57

Look at people for an example, but then make sure to do things your way. Surround yourself with positive people.

Queen Latifah

DAY 58

That's my gift. I let that negativity roll off me like water off a duck's back. If it's not positive, I didn't hear it. If you can overcome that, fights are easy.

George Foreman

DAY 59

In every day, there are 1,440 minutes. That means we have 1,440 daily opportunities to make a positive impact.

Les Brown

DAY 60

Coming together is a beginning;
keeping together is progress; working
together is success.

Henry Ford

DAY 61

Try not to become a man of success, but rather try to become a man of value.

Albert Einstein

DAY 62

Action is the foundational key to all success.

Pablo Picasso

DAY 63

Success is a lousy teacher. It seduces smart people into thinking they can't lose.

Bill Gates

DAY 64

Always do your best. What you plant now, you will harvest later.

Og Mandino

DAY 65

I've failed over and over and over again in my life and that is why I succeed.

Michael Jordan

DAY 66

It's not what you look at that matters,
it's what you see.

Henry David Thoreau

DAY 67

If you have no critics you'll likely have no success.

Malcolm X

DAY 68

Having soon discovered to be great, I must appear so, and therefore studiously avoided mixing in society, and wrapped myself in mystery, devoting my time to fasting and prayer.

Nat Turner

DAY 69

God lets you be successful because he trusts you that you will do the right thing with it. Now, does he get disappointed often? All the time, because people get there and they forget how they got it.

Steve Harvey

DAY 70

One secret of success in life is for a man to be ready for his opportunity when it comes.

Benjamin Disraeli

DAY 71

The size of your success is measured by the strength of your desire; the size of your dream; and how you handle disappointment along the way.

Robert Kiyosaki

DAY 72

Stop being average. You're not even good. You were born to be great.

Eric Thomas

DAY 73

The secret of getting ahead is getting started.
Mark Twain

DAY 74

No matter what people tell you, words and ideas can change the world.

Robin Williams

DAY 75

You have no choices about how you lose, but you do have a choice about how you come back and prepare to win again.

Pat Riley

DAY 76

There's too much darkness in the world. Everywhere you turn, someone is tryin' to tear someone down in some way; everywhere you go, there's a feeling of inadequacy, or a feeling that you're not good enough. I want to bring a certain light to the world.

Alicia Keys

DAY 77

Most people should be talking about how Floyd Mayweather is a great undefeated future Hall of Famer that's his own promoter and that works extremely hard to get to where he's at. Instead, all you hear is hate and jealous remarks from critics who criticize me and, you know, most of the time, the people that criticize me can't do what I can do.

Floyd Mayweather, Jr.

DAY 78

Develop an attitude of gratitude, and give thanks for everything that happens to you, knowing that every step forward is a step toward achieving something bigger and better than your current situation.

Brian Tracy

DAY 79

I cannot think that we are useless or God would not have created us. There is one God looking down on us all. We are all the children of one God. The sun, the darkness, the winds are all listening to what we have to say.

Geronimo

DAY 80

I can't change the direction of the wind, but I can adjust my sails to always reach my destination.

Jimmy Dean

DAY 81

Education is the most powerful weapon which you can use to change the world.

Nelson Mandela

DAY 82

True wisdom comes to each of us
when we realize how little we
understand about life, ourselves, and
the world around us.

Socrates

DAY 83

Life is not a problem to be solved, but a reality to be experienced.

Soren Kierkegaard

DAY 84

To live is to suffer, to survive is to find
some meaning in the suffering.
Friedrich Nietzsche

DAY 85

Most folks are as happy as they make up their minds to be.

Abraham Lincoln

DAY 86

A hero is someone who has given his or her life to something bigger than oneself.

Joseph Campbell

Day 87

The best and most beautiful things in the world cannot be seen or even touched - they must be felt with the heart.

Helen Keller

Day 88

People often say that motivation doesn't last. Well, neither does bathing - that's why we recommend it daily.

Zig Ziglar

DAY 89

Worry never robs tomorrow of its sorrow, it only saps today of its joy.

Leo Buscaglia

DAY 90

Just as treasures are uncovered from the earth, so virtue appears from good deeds, and wisdom appears from a pure and peaceful mind. To walk safely through the maze of human life, one needs the light of wisdom and the guidance of virtue.

Buddha

AFTERWORD

Thank you all for reading this book, I hope you have enjoyed it.

15 Day Goals

30 Day Goals

60 Day Goals

90 Day Goals